CW01654012

The best guide of

KOS

with 123 coloured photographs

ATHENS

Publisher:
Stelios Kontaratos
Iakovos Kontaratos
Texts:
Daskalaki Eleni
Photographs:
L. Chapsis, G. Vdokakis, P. Voukouris
A. Rodopoulos, K.Kondos
Artistic Editing:
N. Vagias
Translation:
Avraam Loucaides - A-Z Services

32 AEROPIS STR. 118 52 ATHENS
TEL.: (210) 34.50.471 FAX: (210) 34.59.114

ISBN: 960-7439-68-6

KOS

The best guide with 123 coloured photographs

HISTORY - CIVILIZATION - ARTS
FOLKLORE - EXCURSIONS - ROAD MAPS

Summer Dream® EDITIONS

CONTENTS

Introduction

The ship approaches the harbour of Kos early in the morning, just after dawn and the castle of the town greets us as it stands majestically under the hot summer sun. We see a tall Turkish minaret far in the horizon and as we get closer and closer, the scenery becomes more and more attractive. The graphic harbour with its yachts, the green vegetation that soothes the eyes, the endless blueness of the bay and the outline of the town all welcome us to the island of Hippocrates.

Whoever arrives at the airport in one of the early morning flights is welcomed by the summer host... the dazzling red disk of the sun that lies before the harbour, scattering the darkness and the shadows of the night while filling us with optimism and impatience for the carefree days of our holiday that we will enjoy on Kos.

A brief stopover at one of the many lodgings offered by Kos and then straight to our rendezvous at the beach. The white and silvery sand and the transparent waters along the 112 kilometres of coastline of the island of Kos entice us even more.

Tavernas, "mezedopoleia" (places serving hors d'oeuvres) and ouzeries found in the town and along the beaches will more than satisfy your palatable appetites while at night the dozens of bars and large clubs fill the narrow roads of Kos with their melodies.

This is how you will pass the days and nights on Kos, with the blending of traditional hospitality, natural beauty and cosmopolitan charm on one of the most popular and most beautiful islands of the Dodecanese.

This is basically how we got to know this distinctive island and we fully recommend it, together with all the information and knowledge that we gleaned during our travels, in order that you may enjoy your holidays.

Have a wonderful holiday and enjoy yourselves!

EFI
MARCO POLO
MARIANA

History
Mythology - Antiquity

Kos –as with most of the regions in Greece- has a very long history. The island was inhabited at least four thousand years before the birth of Christ and this can be verified by the Neolithic findings discovered in the Cave of Aspri Petra (White Rock) near the village of Kefalos.

During the initial centuries of the existence of man on the earth, all natural phenomena as well as what we today call civilisation exchanges, were explained through myth making and mythology.

So let us take them one at a time –as easy as this can be

Mosaic floor depicting Coa greeting Asklepios

since we know that the tales of mythology are more complicated than that of the "clue of thread" given by Cretan Princess Ariadne to Theseus in order to help him escape from the Labyrinth. But that is another tale from mythology.

The sacred grounds of the Asklepieion

The mythological birth of the ancient world was depicted by Titanomachy (battle of the Titans) and Gigantomachy (war of the Giants). This concerns the war between the generations of gods that clashed together for domination of the world of the mortals. One of the battles of the Giants took place on Kos, and in fury, Poseidon (the god of the sea) cut off a piece of Kos and threw it at the giant Polyvotis, whom he was chasing.

This piece of land fell into the sea, forming Nisyros. This myth is depicted on a Roman mosaic found today in Kastello on Rhodes.

The many names by which Kos appears throughout history shows the changes of kings, conquerors and peaceful settlements that took place from neighbouring races.

Depiction of the façade of the Asklepieion by the archaeologist Rudolf Herzog

A headless statue of Asklepeion with the demon Telesforo at his feet (2nd C.)

According to one version of mythology, the first mythical king of Kos was Triopas. He and his son Meropas arrived on Kos from the Asia Minor Cape of Triopion that lay opposite. Thus the first inhabitants of the island were called Triopes and Meropes. Being the gallant and competent people that they were, they established the first city on the island, naming it Astypalaia after the daughter of the king.

The successor to Meropas was Triopas II, who was then followed by Meropas II. One of his daughters was called Kos (Coas), for whom the island was named after.

The movement of the different Greek tribes (Carians and Dorians) towards Kos were metaphorically depicted in a myth that links the island to the hero and semi-god Hercules.

Hercules, the illegitimate son of Zeus, landed on Kos when he and his companions were shipwrecked as they were returning from Troy, where he had carried out a valiant deed. Travelling inland, the

beleagued men met the shepherd Antagoras. Hercules asked if he could buy a sheep but the muscular shepherd proposed that they wrestle instead, saying that if he lost, he would give Hercules a sheep free of charge.

Even though he was weary from his hardships, Hercules accepted the challenge and began wrestling with Antagoras. This news soon reached the inhabitants of Astypalea, who hastened to go and observe the confrontation between the two men. Furious about the unfairness of this contest, Hercules' companions joined in and the confrontation soon transformed into an actual battle. At one point, Hercules -exhausted by his adventures- wandered away followed by his companions and he soon found shelter in the house of a Thrakiotissan. He dressed in women's clothes and sought refuge in the mountains, hounded by King Evrypilos. The place where he took refuge was named **Fyxa** (from the word "fygi" meaning escaped), which today is situated near Pyli.

The inhabitants of the region gave refuge to Hercules and helped him in his fight against Evrypilos. During the battle the king's son, Chalkonas, wounded Hercules. Even though he was wounded, Hercules killed Evrypilos and Chalkonas was then declared King of Kos.

An amphora depicting the Gigantomachy (War of the Giants). The god Ares is high in the centre with the Dioscuri around him, and below are the giants (Athens Arch. Museum)

The king then gave his sister Chalkiopi to Hercules to become his wife.

From this union Heracledis Thessalos was born, who later was to become king of the adjacent islands. His sons Antiphos and Pheidippos led the thirty ships that the islands of Kos, Leros and Kalymnos (all known then by the name of **Kalyndres**) –as well as the islands of **Nisyros, Karpathos** and **Kasos**- sent to fight against Troy. Thus began the kingdom of the generation of the Heracleans, with a famous descendent thought to be Hippocrates. This relationship between Kos and the Heracleans has been cryptographed by historians as verification of the close ties between the Coans and Thessaly.

A statue of the goddess Hygeia and Eros, Hypnos

PRE-HISTORIC YEARS

Excavations that have been carried out periodically on Kos have brought to light **pre-historic fossils** that clearly prove that Kos –together with many of the current islands in the Aegean- comprised a section of Aegiidas and was united with the shores of Asia Minor.

During the period of the **Minoan domination** in the Aegean, Kos was an ally of Minos. Traces of a Minoan settlement from Crete have been found in the site of the current town (region of **Seragia**). After the power of the Minoans declined, after 1600 B.C. the Myceneans expanded in the Aegean, and during this period Kos was settled by the Phoenicians, followed later by the Achaeans, who were already dominating the Aegean region.

After the fall of Troy and the end of the Trojan War, in which Kos had as we mentioned before participated with thirty ships, the Homeric doctor

A rectangular burial altar in the Archaeological Museum of Kos

Podalirios sought refuge on the island. **Podalirios** was the son of Asklepios, who established the worshipping of Asklepios on the island.
In 1104 B.C. -80 years after the Trojan War- the **Dorians appeared** in the islands of the Aegean and along the shores of Asia Minor. It was natural that this Dorian admixture would affect the Kosians, with the Dorian dialect and written language dominating, together with their morals and customs and political organisation. It was obvious that Kos held a significant place among the other Dorian cities by its participation in the Dorian Hexapolis (Ialysos, Kameiros, Lindos, Knidos, Alikarnassos and Kos), whose members congregated at the Sanctuary of Apollo in Triopio in Asia Minor for religious festivals and sports events.
In remembrance of the victory of a Kosian athlete at one of the athletic meetings, the Kosians minted silver coins between 470-450 B.C. that depicted a discus thrower and a tripod on the one side and a crab on the other. However, despite the intense Dorian influence, Kos also showed significant Ionian influences during the ancient years. Finally, the political scene during this period developed gradually -as in all Greek cities- from a monarchy to a democracy with emphasis on the powers of the Municipal church - the greatest institution in a democratic state.

CLASSICAL YEARS

At the end of the **6th Century B.C.** the Persians moved westwards, conquering the Greek cities in Asia Minor and prepared themselves to invade mainland Greece. The islands in the Aegean, including Kos, soon fell under their dominance.
Even though relations between Kos and the Persians

Dionysos, Satyr, Pan and Erotideas

were good initially, the fact that they were forced to send ships against Athens at Platees and at Salamina brought them into conflict, so Kos was therefore relieved when they were delivered from the Persians and incorporated into the **First Athenian Alliance**. But gradually Kos –together with the other members of the Alliance- lost its autonomy and the Alliance was soon transformed into the Athenian Principality.

During the **Peloponnesian War** (431-404 B.C.) the Spartans attacked Kos, causing much damage and destruction. The final defeat of the Athenians caused a civil war on Kos since the democratic and monarchical factions could no longer co-exist together.

A catastrophic **earthquake** in 412 B.C. completed the destruction of the island. During the final years of the Peloponnesian War, Kos did not have stable relations with its allies, so after the earthquake the Spartan Admiral Astyochos looted **Astypalea**, which was situated on the north-eastern side of the island, and the following year the city was again besieged by the Athenian Alkiviadis. But many of its inhabitants had moved to a nearby island, giving it the name of their city, and this island today is of course Astypalea.

An ancient capital

HIPPOCRATES The father of Medicine

Hippocrates was the most significant of the ancient Asklepieions (physicians) and the first to systematically classify medicine and transform it into a science.

According to tradition, Hippocrates was born in the ancient capital of the island, Astypalea, in **460 B.C.** He was a descendent of the Asklepieions from his father Heracledis and a descendent of the Heracledions from his mother Phainaretis. His education –which was

the best available at that period- began on Kos and then continued in Asklepieion in Knidos.

He travelled to Athens, Thrace, Skythia, Macedonia, Thasos, Thessaly, Ionia and Egypt, each time enriching his knowledge concerning nature and the sciences during his travels. When he returned to Kos, he headed the **medical school** on Kos and began teaching and research.

Despite the fact that one of his first concerns was to organise medicine on a scientific basis, his studies in philosophy would not allow him to permanently separate these two sciences.

The diagnosis and application of his treatments were amazing for that period. However, Hippocrates' most significant contribution to medicine was probably employing this science to the service of mankind – determining the ethical and humane duties of a doctor and the **Hippocratic Oath** are still accepted and applied even today in the 21st Century.

Hippocrates died in Larisa at the age of either 104 or 109. The international medical world honoured him one more time when they established the **International Hippocratic Institute** on Kos in October 1960. The objective of this Institute is the communication between all those involved in the science of medicine, the rivalry between doctors, the honouring of medical papers and findings and the publishment of the works of Hippocrates.

HELLENISTIC YEARS

The existence of six municipalities on the island became known during the **Hellenistic years.** It seems that these municipalities – which were created at the same time as the new city of Kos- succeeded older settlements, following the models of the Municipalities of Athens and Rhodes. The Municipality of Isthmioton near the current village of Kephalos, is associated with the ancient capital of

The famous plane tree of Hippocrates with the stone columns next to it

THE HIPPOCRATIC OATH

1. Όμνυμι Απόλλωνα ιητρόν και Ασκληπιόν και Υγείαν και Πανάκειαν και Θεούς πάντας τε και πάσας ίστορας ποιεύμενος, επιτελέα ποιήσειν κατά δύναμιν και κρίσιν εμήν όρκος τόνδε και ξυγγραφήν τήνδε.

2. Ηγήσασθαι μεν τον διδάξαντα με την τέχνην ταύτην ίσα γενέτησιν εμοίσι, και βίου κοινώσασθαι και χρεών χρηίζοντι μετάδοσιν ποιήσασθαι και γένος το εξ αυτού αδελφεοίς ίσον επικρινέειν άρρεσι, και διδάξειν την τέχνην ταύτην, ην χρηίζουσι μανθάνειν, άνευ μισθού και ξυγγραφής.

3. Παραγγελίης τε και ακροήσιος και της λοιπής απάσης μαθήσιος μετάδοσιν ποιήσασθαι υιοίσι τε εμοίσι και τοίσι του εμέ διδάξαντος και μαθηταίσι συγγεγραμμένοις τε και ωρκισμένοις νόμω ιατρικώ, άλλω δε ουδενί.

4. Διατήμασι τε χρήσομαι επ' ωφελείη καμνόντων κατά δύναμιν και κρίσην εμήν, επί δηλήσει δε και αδικίη είρξειν.

5. Ου δώσω δε ουδέ φάρμακον ουδενί αιτηθείς θανάσιμον, ουδέ υφηγήσομοι ξυμβουλίην τοιήνδε ομοίως δε ουδέ γυναικί πεσσόν φθόριο δώσω.

6. Αγνώς δε και οσίως διατηρήσω δίον τον εμόν και τέχνην την εμήν.

7. Ου τεμέω δε ουδέ μη λιθιώντας, εκχωρήσω δε εργάτησιν ανδράσιν πρήξιος τήσδε.

8. Ες οικίας δε οκόσας αν εσίω, εσελεύσομαι επ' ωφελείη καμνόντων, εκτός εών πάσης αδικίης εκουσίης και φθορίης τη τε άλλης και αφροδισίων έργων επί τε γυναικίων σωμάτων και ανδρίων, ελευθέρων τε και δούλων.

9. Α δ' αν εν θεραπείη η ίδω ή ακούσω ή και άνευ θεραπείης κατά βίον ανθρώπων, α μη χρη ποτέ εκλαλέεσθαι έξω, σιγήσομαι, άρρητα ηγεύμενος είναι τα τοιαύτα.

10. Όρκον μεν ούν μοι τόνδε επιτελέα ποιέοντι και μη ξυγχέοντι είη επαύρασθαι και βίου και τέχνης, δοξαζομένω παρά πάσιν ανθρώποις ες τον αεί χρόνων. παραβαίνοντι δε και επιορκέοντι, τανατία τουτέων.

1. I swear by Apollo Physician and Asclepius and Hygia and Panaceia and all the gods and goddesses, making them my witnesses, that I will fulfil according to my ability and judgement this oath and this covenant:

2. To hold him who has taught me this art as equal to my parents and to live my life in partnership with him, and if he is in need of money to give him a share of mine, and to regard his offspring as equal to my brothers in male lineage and to teach them this art -if they desire to learn it- without fee and covenant.

3. To give a share of precepts and oral instruction and all the other learning to my sons and to the sons of him who has instructed me and to pupils who have signed the covenant and have taken an oath according to the medical law, but to no one else.

4. I will apply dietetic measures for the benefit of the sick according to my ability and judgement; I will keep them from harm and injustice.

5. I will neither give a deadly drug to anybody if asked for it, nor will I make a suggestion to this effect. Similarly I will not give to a woman an abortive remedy.

6. In purity and holiness I will guard my life and my art.

7. I will not use the knife, not even on sufferers from stone, but will withdraw in favour of such men as are engaged in this work.

8. Whatever house I may visit, I will come for the benefit of the sick, remaining free of all intentional injustice, of all mischief and in particular of sexual relations with both female and male people, be they free or slaves.

9. What I may see or hear in the course of the treatment or even outside of the treatment in regard to the life of men, which on no account one must spread abroad, I will keep to myself, holding such things shameful to be spoken about.

10. If I fulfil this oath and do not violate it, may it be granted to me to enjoy life and art, being honoured with fame among all men for all time to come; if I transgress it and swear falsely, may the opposite of all this be my lot.

Astypalea. A small Doric temple dedicated to Demeter and dating back to the 5th Century B.C. was discovered near Palatia, beneath the Church of the Panagia of Palatianis, while to the south a small theatre from the Hellenistic era came to light, its altar situated in the centre of the orchestra pit, as well as two Doric chapels. It is said that one of these was dedicated to Asklepieion. The Municipality of Antimachidon was probably situated in the area of Antimachias and was the centre for the worshipping of Hercules. The temple's priest wore women's clothes when he made sacrifices in honour of Hercules, in remembrance of the times when Hercules was disguised as a woman in order to escape from his pursuers after the battle with Antagora. There was a second municipality in the same region called Aigilion.
The Municipality of Alasarniton in the region of Kardamena was the centre for the idolatry of Apollo and Hercules – an annual event carried out by the Dorians.

ASKLEPIOS

Asklepios was the illegitimate son of Apollo and the Thessalian Koronida. Apollo raised his son and taught him the secrets of medicine, which were supplemented by Asklepios studying under the Centaur Chiron in Pylio.

Asklepios became known for his skills in healing all ailments and for relieving the pain suffered by patients. His exceptional skills -which included raising the dead- made him renowned, but this fame attracted the envy of Zeus, who threw a bolt of lightning at Asklepios which killed him.

The secrets of medicine were passed by Asklepios to his children Machaonas, Podaleirios, Iasos, Panakia, Akesos, and Hygeia.

The worshipping of Asklepios spread throughout Greece, with the main sites being Epidavros –where it was established in the beginning of the 5th Century B.C.- and of course Kos.

Thousands of the faithful from all over visited these Asklepieions. These pilgrims firstly made sacrifices to the god and participated in purification ceremonies of atonement, then they could enter the sanctuary where their god appeared before them, giving them the suitable treatment for their ailments. His son Podaleirios was thus the creator of the medical school on Kos.

The Aphrodite Eros Complex

The ancient Municipality of Alention is associated with the region of Pyli. A festival called Thalysia was carried out here in honour of Demeter. Remnants of the Helle-nistic hero Charmylos and his family can be seen in Pyli, including the underground family chamber and parts of the small chapel situated on top of it.

Mycenean graves have also been found in Pyli, while the Byzantium castle in Paliotypi was preceded by a fortified acropolis from the Mycenean era.

The Municipality of Fyxioton was situated in the area of Asfendiou where according to tradition, Hercules took refuge after being pursued. Finally, the centre of the Municipality of Ippioton –between Mastichariou and Zipariou- was situated near the Chapel of Ag. Georgios of Liizou.

A milestone in the island's history was the establi-shment of the new city in 366 B.C. which underwent a great period of acme, mainly through the inflow of patients arriving to be treated at the Asklepieion. The new city had a wonderful street layout, splendid public buildings and churches, sewerage and water works and a large, safe harbour.

The prosperity that the city enjoyed, the filled coffers of its public offices and private individuals as well as its fortifications again attracted the interest of the Athenians on Kos, and they thus included it in the **Second Athenian Alliance,** together with Rhodes.

When the Alliance disbanded, the oligarchic movement assumed control with the support of the tyrant Mavsolou, based in Alikarnassos. In this manner Kos moved away from the influences of Athens.

During the initial years of the domination of **Phillip** and **Alexander**, Kos was liberated in 332 B.C. and – together with the other Greek islands- its course was parallel to

Roman trapezoid that depicts Marsia. The statue of Hermes sitting on a rock and next to him is a ram (Kos Museum)

the **Macedonian hegemony**.

During the period of the successors of the Macedonian Empire created by Alexander in the East, Kos found itself at times being under the domination of Antogonos and at times under Ptolemaion.

Trading flourished on Kos. Wines, aromatic goods and silk materials brought much wealth both to the island in general as well as to various individuals. Impressive public buildings adorned the city and a university was opened, thus giving more impetus to the education and refinement of the inhabitants. Renowned physicians succeeded Hippocrates and in 242 B.C. the sanctity of the Asklepieion was declared.

During this period the celebrating of the **Great Asklepieion** was established every five years, with musicians and athletic games and with the participation of representatives and athletes from all the Greek cities.

Two great poets of the Hellenistic period came to light during this period of prosperity - Theocritus and Herondas, who are linked with Kos.

Monuments that have been preserved from the passing of time

ROMAN YEARS
BYZANTINE PERIOD

Around the end of the 2nd Century B.C. the Roman power began to diffuse into the Hellenistic East, a manifestation that the Greeks were late to perceive. Kos arranged in a timely manner to follow the steps of neighbouring Rhodes by declaring its political allegiance to Rome. In fact, in the **Syrian War** (192-190 B.C.) both Kos and Rhodes fought with Rome against Antiochos.
When the Romans eventually overran Greece, they attached Kos to the Proconsular Province of Asia. The Kosians secured certain privileges such as freedom, Roman nationality for many local residents and maintenance of the sanctity of the Asklepieion. During

Depiction of the ceremony at the Asklepieion

this period a Jewish community was created on Kos and a large number of foreigners originating from the East settled on the island, -due to the positive political climate found on Kos.

After the Roman Empire was divided, Kos -together with the other islands in the Aegean- formed a separate District with Rhodes as its capital. Commercial activities continued and the harbour remained a significant commercial and transportation centre The Roman monuments remind us of the prosperity of Kos during this period.

The economic and cultural prosperity of Kos also continued during the **Byzantine period**, despite the seismic tremors that often visited the island. The **Apostle Paul** was the first Christian to preach the words of the Lord on Kos. In fact, in accordance with a popular legend -which we do not know if it relates to reality- Paul preached Christianity under the shade of Hippocrates' plane tree.

During the first few years the Romans tried to stop the preaching of this new religion and its faithful. The Kosians however were not intimidated and finally, religious tolerance was declared through the signing of the Mediolanon Decree in 313 A.D.

When the Roman Empire was divided into east and west a few years later in 330 A.D., Kos became part of the "**District of the Islands**" in the Eastern Sector with

Rhodes as the capital, which later became the Byzantine Empire.
When the Byzantine Empire flourished, the same applied to its constituents, including the Dodecanese. Thus Kos developed economically wise mainly due to its geographical position that was strategically placed for Byzantine trading.
Another characteristic of this historical period was the continuous raids by pirates and barbaric tribes that domineered the islands of the Aegean. Persians, Saracens, Normans, Visigotthiis and Slavs caused immeasurable damage and terrorised the villages and towns. The Kosians reacted dynamically and courageously after each destructive raid and regathered themselves from the ruins that remained.
Another earthquake in 554 was catastrophic for Kos as it turned nearly every building on the island into ruins.

Venetian building which today houses the Police Station

FRANKISH RULE
TURKISH OCCUPATION PERIOD
RECENT YEARS

The greatest danger however was the Franks, who began travelling eastwards under the guise of the Crusaders. The Crusaders were comprised of different nationalities such as Venetians, Franks and Germans, and finally in 1204 Kos -together with the other lands in the Byzantine Empire- passed under the rule of Baldwin of Flanders.

The division of the Byzantine domains brought Kos under **Venetian** rule in 1302, and two years later to the **Genoese** and finally, in 1314 the Knights of the Order of St. John from Jerusalem occupied Kos. The Knights of St. John were also called the Knights of Rhodes, who formed a strong and dynamic army. They repaired all the old Byzantine castles on the island and fortified the city with a strong castle that still dominates over the ruins of the ancient Hellenistic wall.

The more the Ottoman Empire became stronger, the more the Greek territories were in danger. In fact, after the fall of Constantinople in 1453, raids by Turkish pirates became more frequent and more destructive until finally, in 1523, **the Turks** managed to occupy Kos and the other Dodecanese Islands, thus beginning a difficult and dark period of subjection in the history of the island. The Turkish occupation lasted 390 years and during this period the Knights attempted to retake the island, but they failed. Throughout all these years the inhabitants paid heavy taxes and worked in the large estates that had been given to the Turkish tyrants.

A circular tower from the Medieval fortifications of the city

The Orthodox Church played a leading role among the subjugated people as it was a legitimate and independent religious and administrative body. But in the 18th C. the Kosians participated in the rebellion against the Turks

and after Greece's independence -which was achieved after the **Revolution** in 1821- Kos remained a Turkish province (in accordance with the Protocol of London in 1830) with a preferential administrative status.
In 1912 Italy succeeded Turkey in ruling the island and the Kosians accepted this change with relief, while hoping that the Italians had arrived as liberators. But many years were to pass before the repeated resolutions by the Dodecaneseans and the Greek Government for independence of the Dodecanese Islands was successful, in order that they may finally be united with the remainder of Greece.
But it was only after the Second World War that the Greek flag flew proudly over Kos on March 7th 1948. However, the Italian administration did construct some notable building projects until this period, but they excluded education.

Folklore

Kos has been known since antiquity for its fertile land and plethora of water, which naturally favoured cultivations. The ancients used to say: "That which Kos cannot nourish, Egypt could not nourish as well".
At the beginning of the 20th C. the island's economy was based on agriculture and stock farming. The development of agriculture was verified by the operations of around 20 watermills and dozens of windmills situated near the coastline, and on high ground that was exposed to the wind.
These windmills were built out of stones found locally and with superfluous labour, in accordance with the economic state and the artistry of the miller. The majority were of the "xetrocharis" type and sections were found in the construction-work of the windmill that contained

ancient stones that were used mainly for doorsteps, decorations or even as building elements.

Only a few of the 75 windmills that operated on Kos have remained today. Two of these are situated in the tourist town of Kardamena and only the "**paliomylos**" (old mill) opposite the Castle stands out, while also giving its name to the region. Two more windmills were operating in the south part of the town of Kos up until the earthquake in 1933. One of these contained the coat of arms of the Great **Magistrou D'Ampoise** built into the lintel, dated 1505.

Only in recent years have there been an attempt to preserve the few windmills that have remained –and these have been destroyed- as historically preserved monuments. One operated ten years ago in Kephalos, but today it stands deserted, while another in Antimachia was restored and is now in very good condition and operates as a tourist attraction.

The island's market is housed in a building with arches

Scenic picture of a traditional Kafenio (coffee shop)

Another centuries-old tradition is the **pottery-works** in Kos. Even from way back in antiquity skilled artists made urns, plates, vases, tiles and various other ceramic objects - all of exceptional artistry. Other than individual potters, the island has two companies that still maintain the art of pottery, as well as a traditional workshop near the village of Platanos.

CHRONICLES OF KOS

In the book "Athinaika, Attikobiotika and Dodekanisiaka 1815-1980" ("Athenian, Attica-Boeotia and Dodecanesean 1815 -1980") written by Prof. P.K. Enepekidis, we can find some remarkable accounts concerning Kos during this period from the travels of the Prussian author Powel Lindau in the Dodecanese at the end of the 19th C. In an observation in the epilogue of the book, the author states that the chief merit of Lindau's travels is that it offers us the capability after one hundred years to compare the Turkish occupied Dodecanese Islands with today's sparkling gems in the Aegean, and it is therefore actual facts.

One of the more interesting reports concerning Kos is

that concerning **Hippocrates' plane tree**: "On Kos -the birthplace of the greatest physician and the renowned painter of antiquity: Hippocrates and Apelles- there is a unique tourist site: a huge plane tree, the biggest of its kind in the world, with its competitors in Prussia and in Bougioukdere (Makri Rema in Constantinople) not even close with respect to its size.

It is exceptionally tall – I estimate it to be approximately 20-30 meters high. But the circumference of its trunk and the expansion of its branches are almost unbelievable. Its trunk, which has some hollows but no cracks -so it looks compact in contrast to the time-ravaged and cracked trunks of other gigantic plane trees- is not less than 16 meters, while the length of its branches reach 30 meters.

The complete square that was formed around the very old tree -together with the mosque and the town hall- is shaded by the branches of this one plane tree, which is still blooming and is in perfect condition, shining with its wonderful green colour. The residents of Kos are trying in the most laudable manner to protect and preserve their tree, which to them is the sanctuary of their town.

The traditional art of pottery continues and today

The heavy branches of the tree (which each one in itself constitutes a huge horizontally growing tree) are supported by two compact stone poles whose ends are buried in the earth, while the lighter branches are

supported by thick beams. The foot of the tree is encircled by a barrier up to the height of a man so that its roots are protected from vandalism.
A stand has therefore been erected around the plane tree and a person can climb onto it via ancient marble steps. A huge horse's head has been placed on the stand for decorative purposes - a bas relief made of marble which probably dates back to the great artistic period in the past.
The residents of Kos have characterised this strange, wonderful, exquisite and one of a kind ancient plane tree

Do not miss the opportunity to enjoy fresh fish straight from the Greek seas

as Hippocrates' tree and they swear that their eminent fellow-countryman -who was born in 460 B.C.- had planted it.
Even if the botanists with their clearheaded knowledge smile knowingly when they hear these childish fantasies, it is still touching that the Kosians honour the memory of their fellow-countryman through the most beautiful monument given to them by Nature – a monument that resurrects itself every Spring.
An interesting note on the plane tree is that it is said that Hippocrates used to sit under the shady tree and write his notes while seeing his patients. Experts maintain that of course this does not refer to the same tree but rather to offshoots of the original tree.

The fishermen's nets dry out under the blazing sun

In the same book Professor Enepekidis refers to Kos as an openair archaeological museum a characterisation that describes perfectly this unique historically interesting town and he goes on to paraphrases Lindau:
"There is a specific open area near the plane tree oh happy Kos! Everything is situated near the plane tree- where the fortuitous findings of antiquity have collected: fragments of statues, columns, etc.".

MEMENTOES OF KOS

You will be able to find and buy the exceptionally local delicacy -the little tomatoes in syrup- in the **town's market** and in various shops. This preserved syrupy sweet is found only on Kos.

Tasty delights from the local specialities that offer one more enjoyable memento to your holidays

Preserved syrupy sweets are an old Greek tradition. Every year the housewives - mostly in the past but still continued today- prepare different syrupy sweets that are preserved for many months in sealed glass jars. These are offered to guests on a small plate accompanied by a glass of cold water... a real treat throughout the year!

In order to prepare and to preserve this

wonderful sweet throughout the year, you should do the following: Place these syrupy sweets in glass jars that have previously been placed in boiling water in order to sterilise them and then thoroughly dried. The jars are stored in a cool and dark place or in the refrigerator. If the sweet has granulated, we re-boil it for a few minutes, adding a little glucose. If mould has collected on the surface, we remove the upper part and throw it away, and we then reboil the remainder for a few minutes until the syrup becomes firm again.

Small tomatoes

1 kg small tomatoes (green and unripe)
1 kg sugar
2 1/2 cups water
2 teaspoons lemon juice
6 pieces of cloves
Whole almonds (white)
Lime water*

1. Dip the small tomatoes into boiling water and then peel them carefully. Make a small cut along the side of the stalk and press lightly so that the seeds come out.
2. Place them in lime-water for 1 hour. Strain them and wash them many times in order to remove the lime and then place them on kitchen paper to drain.
3. To make the syrup, boil water and sugar in a pot for 5′, add the tomatoes, lemon juice and cloves and boil for about 10′. If froth forms, remove it carefully with a skimmer.
4. Remove the pot from the fire and leave it standing for 1 day.
5. On the following day remove the cloves and the tomatoes from the pot. Boil the syrup a little longer so that it becomes firm and place an almond into the cuts of each tomato. Put them again into the syrup, let them cool and then put into jars.

* To prepare the lime-water, mix 2 soup spoons slaked lime in 2 litres of water and pass through a fine sieve. Cover the tomatoes with the lime- water and leave for 1 hour. The lime-water prevents the tomatoes from breaking up during boiling.
* However, you can omit the lime-water, but you must then choose the small tomatoes carefully and not stir them during boiling, but rather move the pot with care.

ΚΩΣ (Πόλη)
KOS (City)

(train, blue)	ΤΡΕΝΟ ΓΙΑ ΑΣΚΛΗΠΙΕΙΟ	TRAIN TO ASKLEPIEIO	7.	ΠΥΡΟΣΒΕΣΤΙΚΗ	FIRE DEPARTMENT
(train, green)	ΤΡΕΝΟ (ΓΥΡΟΣ ΤΗΣ ΠΟΛΗΣ)	TRAIN (CITY TOUR)	8.	ΚΤΕΛ	BUS STATION
■	ΤΡΑΠΕΖΑ	BANK	9.	ΤΑΞΙ	TAXI
1.	ΑΣΤΥΝΟΜΙΑ	POLICE	10.	ΠΛΑΤΑΝΟΣ ΙΠΠΟΚΡΑΤΗ	HIPPOCRATIS TREE
2.	ΤΑΧΥΔΡΟΜΕΙΟ	POST OFFICE	11.	ΔΕΑΣ ΔΗΜΟΤΙΚΗ ΣΥΓΚΟΙΝΩΝΙΑ	LOCAL BUS
3.	ΛΙΜΕΝΑΡΧΕΙΟ	PORT AUTHORITY	12.	ΕΠΑΡΧΕΙΟ	PREFECTURE
4.	ΔΗΜΑΡΧΕΙΟ	TOWN HALL			
5.	ΑΡΧΑΙΟΛΟΓΙΚΟ ΜΟΥΣΕΙΟ	ARGHEOLOGICAL MUSEUM			
6.	Ε.Ο.Τ. (ΕΛΛΗΝΙΚΟΣ ΟΡΓΑΝΙΣΜΟΣ ΤΟΥΡΙΣΜΟΥ)	GREEK ORGANIZATION OF TOURISM (E.O.T.)			

The town of Kos

(Excerpts from the book by the author Powel Lindau)

"We left Alikarnassos at 10 in the morning and after ninety minutes we reached the neighbouring island of Kos. The wide bay does not offer any safety to the ships. And here again, of the ruins reminiscent of a castle from the years of the knights, only the strong jagged walls still remain.
Heading south, we reach the buildings of the town that are all at sea level along the coastline. A park where the trees unusually have thick foliages lies next to the sea, giving an exceptionally pleasant note to the town.
The land is fertile but the island is poor. It has 8,000 - 9,000 inhabitants of which 2,500 live in the town. The wide avenue is lined with fine cypress trees, offering shade and a pleasing note. The complete picture is that of a quiet and remarkable mainland market town.
The whole town is built inside the castle. Only a few buildings can be seen to have been derived from the era of the Knights. They have the characteristic entrance with the coat of arms either next to or above the gate with the

The coastal road of Kos

The Medieval Gate of Forou in Elephtheria square

ΕΙΣΟΔΟΣ ΠΡΟΣ
ΠΛΑΤΑΝΟΝ ΚΑΙ
ΑΓΟΡΑΝ
FOR
TREE
AGORA

501

early **Gothic archway**, but it should be noted that many of them have become detached and you can only see the empty space on the slate."

The gate of the Castle

This excerpt describes what the Prussian author Powel Lindau saw when he arrived on Kos during his travels around the Dodecanese at the end of the last century. It was published in the book "Athinaika, Attikobiotika and Dodekanisiaka 1815-1980" ("Athenian, Attica-Veotia and Dodecanesean 1815-1980") written by Prof. P.K. Enepekidis and published by Oceanida Publishers.

And today, when the visitor arrives by sea the first thing he will see is the harbour with the **Venetian Castle** of the Knights – a barrier against the wind-swept sea and aspiring conquerors. The Castle with its double walls or enceintes and moat was built towards the end of the 14th C. by the Knights of the Order of St. John, using materials from the foundations of the old fortress and the walls.

The old unassailable turrets of the Castle are swamped by tourists of all nationalities who gaze spellbound at the Aegean Sea and the Turkish shores that are just a stone's throw away on the one side and the picturesque town of Kos on the other. As for the turrets with their embrasures, bastions and cornices, that which personifies the era of the castle is the bastion facing the harbour (south-west).

The **south gate** of the Castle is linked to the old town by an **arched bridge** which crosses the **Avenue of the Palm-Trees**. During the period of acme this wide road -which today is one of the most scenic spots in the town- was the moat of the Castle that was filled with seawater in order to keep the enemy at bay.

Various ancient artefacts, coat of arms (among them the coat of arms of the Great Magistrou D'Ampoise), parts of the old fortress and doors adorn the interior of the Castle. A small section of the Castle has been transformed into an

The Avenue of the Palm Trees that leads to the Castle

The Ancient Race Track - The Roman Baths

Views of the Castle

open-air theatre where during August various musical and theatrical performances are given in an imposing setting - all within the framework of the cultural events presented by the Municipality of Kos. Another external gate -the "Porta tou Forou" or Gate of Forou (from the Latin word 'forum' meaning market)- leads us to the ancient market place.

The town of Kos is truly an open-air **archaeological** and **historical museum.** As we stroll along its narrow alleys, the picture that we see changes as the eras changed: the **monuments of antiquity** that are scattered throughout the town blend harmoniously with the buildings from the **Middle-Ages,** such as the **Turkish mosque** and its slender minarets with the new and excellently planned town. This therefore gives the visitor a clear and graphic narration of Kos' course throughout the centuries.

A meeting point and probably the most scenic corner in the town is the Plateia (Square) of the Plane Tree of Hippocrates. This concerns a gigantic tree with a circumference of around 12 m, where according to

The Lotzia Mosque

The Ancient Agora (Market

The Roman Odeion (2nd C.)

tradition, Hippocrates sat under its shade while examining his patients.

Of course, even though we are talking about the oldest tree in Europe, **the plane tree** that we now see is not the same tree way back in antiquity, but rather an offshoot of the original. The huge and heavy branches of the tree are supported by stone pillars and modern constructions, while its base is enclosed by a protective fence in order to

safeguard the roots.
During the Turkish occupation period, an ancient sarcophagus was placed beneath the plane tree in which running water collected. This sarcophagus was used as a water tank for the Lotzia Mosque and we can still discern the Arabic writing with the date inscribed on it, when the Mosque was erected by Gazi Hassan Pasha (1786).
Ancient materials were also used in building the Mosque, as well as seven marble columns from the **"Seven Steps** Church of Ag. Ioannis" (St. John).

The Defterdar Mosque

The paved "Plateia" (square) with the plane tree and the bougainvillaea, the gate of the Castle, the open-air painters and the music streaming from the small, vibrant orchestras that entertain customers in the neighbouring café-bars, together with the **ancient market** that spreads out on the other side of the square, all blend together to compose a unique picture that the visitor will find unforgettable.
Another paved alley -which the locals delightfully call "Exarchia" due to the dozens of bars that are found here, one next to the other- passes under the Forou Gate and

ends up at **Plateia Eleftheria (Liberty Square).**
Here we will come across one more monument from the Turkish occupation period – the **Defterdar Mosque.**

The Road of the Bars

This mosque is used for worshipping by those Turks that still live on Kos and is open every Friday for the faithful and for visitors. Up until a few years ago, every Friday the Kosians would wake up to the voice of the muezzin calling on the faithful to pray.

Diagonally opposite the **Archaeological Museum** is the Club, which has on its façade a sign containing the verses from the Greek National Anthem and the date when Kos was united with the rest of Greece.

On the opposite side of the plateia stands the impressive Municipal Agora (market) building, which every morning fills up with fresh juicy fruit and vegetables and the air vibrates with the shouts of the locals as they select their goods, together with the pungent aromas of the aromatic

The Club

herbs. Hundreds of locals and visitors visit the Agora every day and come out holding bulging bags filled with delicious Kosian "goodies". The Archaeological Museum is directly opposite and houses the findings that came to light from the excavations carried out on Kos from the turn of the century until today. These findings date from the Hellenistic up to the post-Roman periods.

Among the impressive findings, the one that stands out is the imposing statue of Hippocrates. This is a portraitist statue, probably from the post-Hellenic period, that is a copy of the classical model found in the Odeion.

A **statue of Hermes** sitting on a rock stands out among the artefacts from the Roman years, which had been found in the House of the Europa Mosaic. You should also look out for the small Persephone that is sited directly opposite the statue of her mother Demeter. In her hands she holds two torches that symbolise the six months she lives in the darkness of Hades.

Finally, the statues from the Roman period situated in the atrium are also impressive. **Artemis**, **Asklepieios** and **Hygeia**, as well as the **Dionysos** and **Satyr** Complex, stand out for their aesthetic lines and their excellent workmanship. The mosaic

Inscription showing the date when Kos united with Greece

that we admire on the floor depicts with great detail the arrival of Asklepieios on Kos and dates back to the 3rd Century A.D. All these were discovered in the House of the Europa Mosaic.

Marble face depicting a lion (Arch. Museum)

Statue of the goddess Aphrodite (2nd C.)

The scenic alleyways of the old town are on your right-hand side (looking at the Agora). Little, narrow roads, well-kept old houses with blooming flowerpots and dozens of tourist shops which spread out their wares before the amazed eyes of the visitors. Ifestou and Apellou Streets are the hub of all activities in the old town. The roads are filled day and night with people buying souvenirs and gifts from Kos.

Strolling along we will also meet **early Christian** and more **recent churche**s with notable frescos and iconostases. Among the **Medieval churches** that stands out are the Church of the Panagia tis Gorgoepikoou or Gorgopigi, the Church of Ag. Ioannis tou Navklirou, the Church of Ag, Ioannis tou Vaptistou (St. John the Baptist), the Church of Ag. Constantinou and the Church of the Panagia tis Katevatis, as well as the Chapel of the Panagia tis Tsoukkalarias in the area of Ambavri. Most of these old churches are situated around the ancient Agora.

Of the more recent churches found inside the town, the one that is worth visiting is Ag. Paraskevi next to Plateia Elefterias.

ARCHAEOLOGICAL SITES

Other than the imposing Castle and the charmness of the old town, a visitor arriving on Kos for the first time will certainly be impressed by the archaeological sites scattered inside the town.

According to sources, the homonymous ancient capital of the island was one of the most beautiful coastal towns in the ancient world. Those buildings that adorned Kos during the Hellenistic years were the theatre, the prytaneum, the gymnasium and the ancient agora buildings that played a double operational and decorative role.

Its perimeter was 4 kilometres with a separate fortification for the harbour. Some sections of the ancient wall dating back to the 4th Century B.C. were discovered in excavations carried out at the harbour. The catastrophic earthquake in 1933 gave the excuse to German and Italian archaeologists to carry out more intensive excavations in the town of Kos, and since there were many monuments, the excavations were divided into zones.

EASTERN ZONE

The complete area around the harbour of the Medieval town was examined and the monuments that came to light

The coastal road to Psalidi

The eastern entrance to the ancient wall

became known as the harbour excavations or the **ancient Agora** excavations, and are all included in the eastern zone. A large section of the wall (80 m by 2.5 m high) built with large stones is discernible. The eastern arm that protected the harbour began from the external side of the wall.

All those buildings necessary for the harbour to operate as well as the churches -which faced the harbour- were sited outside the wall. The eastern arm acted as a brace for an **impressive colonnade** 50 meters in length, dating back to the 4th or 3rd Century B.C., with a row of rooms. During the Roman era the greater part of the colonnade was restored and it was later covered by an early Christian Basilica by Limenos. In modern times the baptismal font of the Basilica was called the "Seven Steps of Ag. Ioannis".

A small chapel –possibly dedicated to Hercules- and mosaic floors in the rooms next to the sanctuary dating back to the 3rd Century B.C. were also discovered. Other findings from temples and sanctuaries belong to the Aphrodision or the **Sanctuary of Pandimou** and Pontias Aphrodite.

The Agora, built right next to the harbour in order to facilitate trading, was -in accordance with very recent findings- a building 80 m wide with a length of about 300 m. An impressive stairway leads from the road to the internal yard. Two columns that have been restored form a type of portico. It is estimated that the first construction of the Agora was between the 4th and 3rd Centuries B.C., while the few pieces from the buildings that have been preserved clearly show many construction periods.

WESTERN ZONE

The **Thermes in the harbour** is comprised of a circular hall with porticoes and is situated on the corner of Omiros and Irodotou Streets. The northern Thermes was found along 31st March Street, dating back to between the 4th and 3rd Centuries B.C. Here the archaeologist's pickaxe discovered a remarkable inscription detailing the worshipping regulations of "Enagoniou Hermes"

The ruins of the **ancient Stadium were** discovered south-west of the northern Thermes. In 1900 the German archaeologist Herzog discovered the "afesis" of the Stadium; i.e. the specially formed starting point for the runners.

The western zone of the excavations includes the Hellenistic Gymnasium (i.e. athletics gym) known as "**Xysto**". The Gymnasium was thus named from the habit of the athletes to scratch (xisoun) their bodies in order to clean it from the oil

Main road from the Hellenistic period

they anointed themselves before the races began. A row of 17 restored columns from the ancient Gymnasium are an impressive sight. There was a tank in the middle of the Gymnasium where athletes could wash themselves, and the western Thermes was adjacent for the same reason.

The ancient "Xysto" Gymnasium

A paved road –**Decumanus Maximus**- 10.5 metres wide with broad pavements and arcades bisects the town, crossing a second road – the Cardo. There were many Roman buildings on both sides of the road, while complex sewerage and drainage systems were also discovered beneath both roads.

To the east of the **Cardo** we'll come across a charming restored building - the 3rd C. Thermes **Nymfeo** or Forica. When the building was first discovered, its elegance initially led archaeologists to the conclusion that this was a sanctuary dedicated to the nymphs, but it was finally determined that the building was a luxury public toilet.

There are various ancient ruins north of the Decumanus, including the **House of the Europa Mosaic.** To the left of the yard a 3rd C. mosaic floor was discovered in a small hall, depicting a nude Europe being held by the throat and the side of a bull. Many statues have been found here, including those of Asklepieion, Artemis and Hygeia, which we can see and admire in the Archaeological Museum.

Opposite the Gymnasium is the **Roman Odeion,** built in the 2nd C., which has been well preserved. The concave opening has nine marble rows that have been restored, a landing and then another five rows made of granite. The lower stands made of marble were for the more "respectable" citizens while the higher stand made of stone was for the remaining spectators. Other sections that were also saved are the floor of the proscenium and the wings, as well as the orchestra pit.

CENTRAL ZONE

The main artefact found in the central excavation zone is the **Casa Romana,** to the right of Grygoriou 5th Street. This is a 3rd C. Roman villa built over the ruins of a Hellenistic house, where wonderful mosaics were discovered.

The villa is Pompeii style with 36 rooms and 3 atriums or internal atria yards with small tanks in the middle, together with a plethora of adornments. In the hallway of the first atrium we can discern a fountain which at one time had a small statue of Asklepieion, while an exquisite

The tank and mosaic in the Atrium of the mansion

mosaic depicting sea animals was found on the floor of an adjacent hall. This latter is now in the Archaeological Museum.

In the second atrium the walls are covered with marble, and mosaic covers the floor around the tank, depicting dolphins and a sea-nymph on a sea-horse.

The third atrium is the largest, bordered by double and single rows of pillars in an arrangement called "rodiaki stoa". The rooms have mosaic and wall murals.

We come across the ruins of the **Central Thermes** outside Casa Romana, with the **ruins of Dionysos** altar lying to the north-east. The temple, which dates back to the 2nd C., was built with white and grey-blue marbles.

In finishing our tour of the archaeological "wealth" on Kos, we now owe it to ourselves to enjoy a relaxing stroll through the nightlife on Kos. Twilight along the shores of **Kountourioti** now takes centre stage. Both locals and visitors enjoy their walk with the berthed yachts and excursion boats on the one side and the restaurants and cafeterias on the other.

As we walk along the sea road just after the Castle, we will come across a wonderful **Venetian building** that is somewhat neglected, which houses the police and the tourist police.

As soon as the sun falls, the town comes alive, the lights from the cafeterias, tavernas and bars cover the sea with coloured hues, and the people stay up all night in order to enjoy the vibrant nightlife on Kos.

External view of the Roman mansion Casa Romana

58-59. The Avenue of the Palm Trees and the bridge of the Castle

Kos - Lambi - Psalidi - Thermes Platanos - Asklepieion

1st Route

Kos is an island with a good road network with wide roads and only a few mountainous routes. So in just a few days you can get to know the island from corner to corner, visiting all the wonderful beaches and picturesque villages.

Other than a car or motorcycle -which you can rent- one of the most popular modes of travelling on the island is the bicycle. The straight and almost level roads (with just a few uphills), together with special bicycle lanes on most of the roads, play a catalytic role in your choice of travelling mode.

And do not think that you have to be in pretty good shape so as to bicycle around! Just a couple of kilometres from the centre you will find some attractive beaches with tavernas, cafeterias and beach bars to help you enjoy the rest of your day.

The open Bay of Kos has a north-easterly orientation, which means that when northern and north-easterly winds blow, the beaches have very few high waves. If the waves still bother you, you can enjoy the windless south-westerly beaches, but you will need a car to get there.

To the north of Kos we find **Lambi**, one of the more

cosmopolitan beaches of the town with its hotels, tavernas, water-sports and all other amenities that help to make our holidays more relaxing. Travelling in the opposite direction, we pass the Cape of **Psalidi** and arrive at **Ag. Foka** continuously developing tourist resort.

The beach here -with its dark coloured pebbles and large luxury hotel complexes- also extends for hundreds of meters. In many places the trees reach almost to the sea, thus offering the sunbathers some priceless shade.

We reach **Thermes** about 1 km after Ag. Foka, where a steep downhill dirt road leads us to the beach. With a little care

Night scene of the harbour of Kos

The old town

you can reach the beach by car, but if you feel like walking, it won't take more than 10 minutes.
A small but beautiful beach with its dark coloured pebbles welcomes us, and a little further down lies the mineral springs along the foot of a high rock. We can see the bubbles of the sulphurous and ferruginous waters in a small sea "pool" -which explains the pungent smell- which is

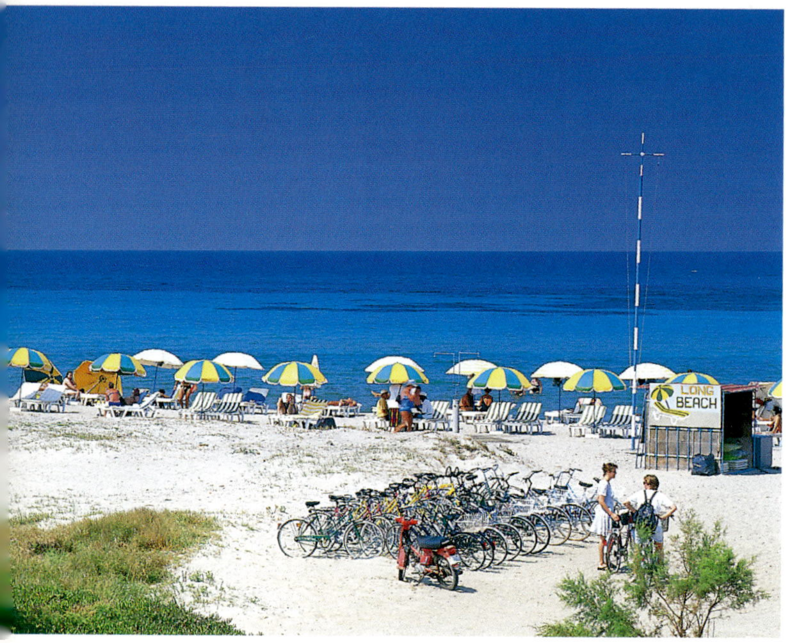

Lambi beach

almost boiling and which is suitable for water-therapy. The sulphurous and ferruginous springs at Thermes especially help those suffering from rheumatism, arthritis and gynaecological disorders.
When we travel inland we must visit the **Asklepieion** – the most famous of all the 300 odd Asklepieions throughout the ancient world. The Asklepieion lies 3.5 km north-west of the town, within a very scenic trip.
As soon as we leave the town behind us, we turn left at the first crossroad, as indicated by the signposts. After about 1 km we meet the settlement of **Platani** (or as it is known in **Turkish... Kermede**).

Thermes with the mineral springs

A huge plane tree hugs the small plateia (square) while its shade covers the tables of the restaurants, which are mainly Turkish. Taking a trip there for lunch in order to taste the delicious Turkish soutzoukakia (meatballs) and the other tasty dishes is a must while you are staying on Kos.

After Platani the road continues under the shade of the tall cypress trees. Once we reach Asklepieion, we can easily realise why its builders chose this site to build this renowned treatment centre. It is built concentrically on a vegetation-filled hill with the town of Kos and its suburbs spreading out serenely at its feet, and even today the visitor is filled with feelings of spiritual euphoria and serenity.

The physicians of the Asklepieion -who also happened to be priests- had adopted the Hippocratic method of diagnosis and treatment. Their symbol was the snake - as it is today- which they honoured thanks to his ability to discover therapeutic herbs.

The cosmopolitan beach of Kahlua

The restored columns of the lower andiras (terrace) of the Asklepieion

Other than treating patients, the Asklepieion also offered sanctuary to whoever asked for it, a prerogative that was maintained even during the difficult historical periods when the island was occupied.
The impressive totality of the Asklepieion was brought to light in 1902 by the German archaeologist R. Herzog, after the site was identified by the Kosian historian Iakovos Zarraftis. The Asklepieion is perched on a hill with three terraces ("andiras" or structures) that are linked together with imposing stone staircases.
The Asklepieion was erected during the first half of the 3rd Century B.C. Earthquakes played a significant role in both its formation and in its development. An earthquake in 155 B.C. was the reason for significant changes to be made, while the earthquake in 554 A.D. was the final blow for the sacred structure, which was crushed by tons of silt.
By this time the Asklepieion had already reached a period of decline because Christianity -which at this time prevailed- was in fierce conflict with the remnants of idolatry. Thus the destruction of the Asklepieion by natural causes was final and decisive and no attempt was made to reconstruct it.
On the first terrace a "stoa" (portico) in the shape of a "Π"

enclosed it on three sides, leaving open only the south side. To the east was a more recent complex of the Roman Thermes (3rd Century A.D.), with porticoes, living quarters for the patients and their families and a plateia (square) with fountains (artistic taps) completing the picture. It is possible that the structures on the first terrace also housed the **medical school**.

There used to be statues in niches on the restored columns that supported the second terrace. What has remained is a stone representation of the god Pan to the left of the staircase leading to the second terrace.

On the second terrace we can see the ruins of a **large altar** dedicated to the Cyparissian Apollo, which is also the oldest structure in the Asklepieion. The altar was built during the 4th Century B.C., but nothing has remained of its sculptured adornments, which have been attributed to the sons of Praxiteles.

To the left and to the right of the altar we can discern the ruins of two smaller temples, while to the west we see the

DIAGRAM OF THE ASKLEPIEION BY THE ARCHAEOLOGIST RUDOLF HERZOG

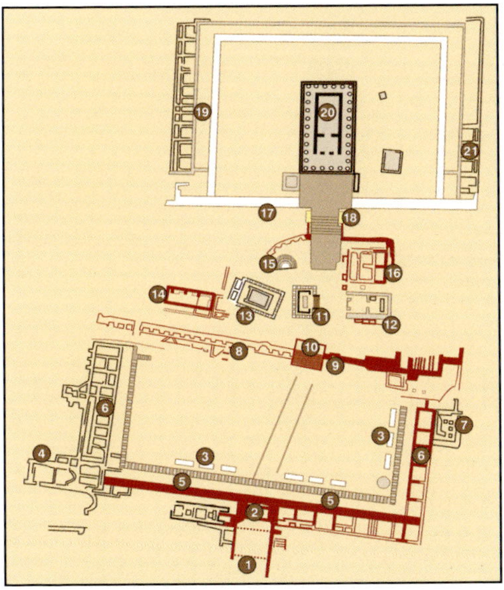

First Terrace
(Andiras)

1. Entrance scale
2. Propylaea
3. Bases (statues)
4. Thermes
5. Stoa (=Portico)
6. Patients Rooms
7. Public Toilet
8. Fragmented Wall
9. Naiskos Xenophontas
10. Scale

Second Terrace

11. Altar of Asklepieion
12. Temple of Asklepieion (Ionic)
13. Temple of Apollo (Corinthian)
14. Club
15. Semi-circular Stand
16. Priests Residence
17. Fragmented Wall
18. Scale

Third Terrace

19. Stoa (=Portico)
20. Large Temple of Asklepieion (Doric)
21. Patients Rooms

restored columns of the Ionian **Temple of Apollo** dating back to the 2nd Century B.C.
The remains of another structure to the south of the altar may possibly be the "avato", an area where the patients waited for Asklepieion to appear in their dreams and cure them.
On the third and highest terrace we can see the great Doric Temple of Asklepieion (2nd Century B.C.); that is, what has remained of it. It seems that this temple was also surrounded by a "Π"-shaped portico, similar to the one on the first terrace.
The Chapel of the Panagia Tarsou was built during the Christian years in the "pronaos" (pretemple) of the ancient temple. It is said that the name of the Panagia (Virgin Mary) evolved from the corruption of the word "tou Alsous" (of the forest), as the Ancient Greeks also worshipped Apollo the Cyparissian (cypress) at the same site!

The small Chapel of Asklepieion

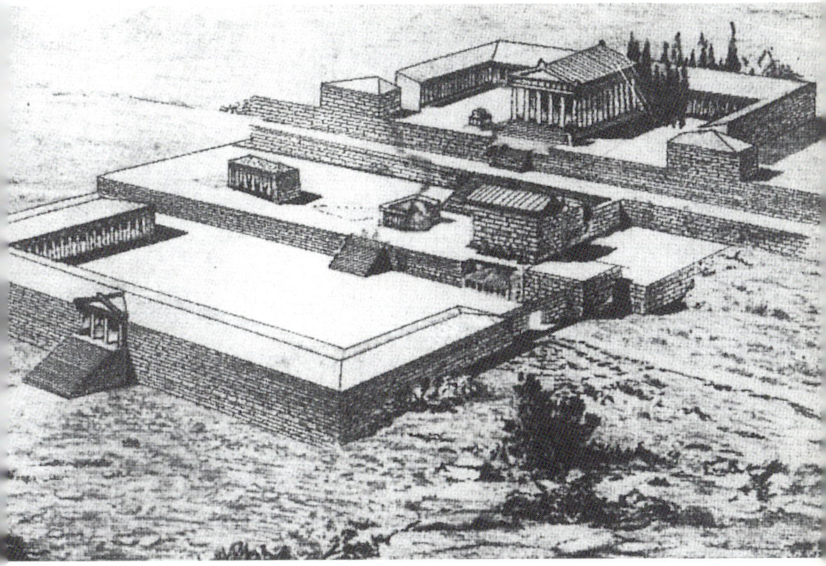

Today we can see only the capital of this very old chapel which was used as the Altar, and on it are inscribed the Christian initials ICXP.

Our tour of the Asklepieion ends here, but the majority of the visitors are in no hurry to leave this hospitable site. Say it is the tall cypress tress that cover us with their freshness, say it is the enchantment of the site with its uninterrupted magnificent view in all directions, Every person that comes here shows that he has the need to sit on one of the eternal rocks and meditate for awhile

Reproduction of the Asklepieion by the archaeologist Rudolf Herzog

68-69. The Corinthian Temple of Apollo (2nd C.)

Kos - Tingaki - Marmari Zipari - Zia

2nd Route

Other than the town and adjacent archaeological sites, Kos also offers wonderful beaches and scenic villages, with **Asfentiou** heading the list as it lies on the green-filled slopes of **Dikeos Mountain.**

Starting from the town of Kos we turn from the plateia with its fountain adorned with the characteristic dolphins and follow the signposts to the airport. For the first few kilometres there is a bicycle lane on the right side of the main road. But on the whole you must be careful of bicycles wherever you go as many tourists prefer to travel around on them, even on longer trips.

Passing by the crossroad for Platani and Asklepieion, we travel through the small hill-top village of **Zipari** and before exiting the village, we turn left towards the villages in the community of Asfentiou.

An uphill road with few bends and rich vegetation leads us to the most beautiful hill-top corner of Kos. **Asfentiou** is comprised of scattered settlements perched on the slopes of Mt. Dikeos. The centre of the community is the village of **Evangelistria**. To the right

A fantastic view from the village of Zia

The Church of Kimisis tis Theotokou in Zia

Traditional house in Lagoudi

and to the left are the villages of **Ag. Dimitrios** or **Haichoutes**, **Asomatos**, **Zia** and **Lagoudi**. The white-washed houses with their flower-filled yards in the villages of Asfentiou stand out for their picturesqueness.

The stone houses of the villages of Asfentiou which are perched on the sides of Mt. Dikeos and adjacent peaks give their inhabitants a valuable means of coolness during the summer heat waves. One of the peaks just above Zia is called **Oromedon**. In Ancient Greek the word "ora" means season, while "meden" means the ruler, the overlord.

The splendid Temple of Analipsis tou Sotira in Zipari

And now during summer, under the overlord of the season -the sun- we together with the village enjoy our holidays on the island of Kos... so rich in beauty and history.

Our eyes luxuriate in the panoramic view of the Asia Minor shores and the islets that lace the Aegean Sea all the way to the endless sandy beaches of Kos

A picturesque church in Asfentiou

that spread out below us.
The view from the historical **Chapel of Dikeos Christos**, which is perched on the precipitous peak of Mt. Dikeos, is just as exciting. If you would like to stroll through the history of the region, just visit the Byzantium chapels found on the slopes of the mountain: The Chapel of **Asomaton Taxiarchon** (11th C.), the early-Christian **Basilica of Ag. Pavlos** and the **Chapels of Kefalovrisi**, Esodia and **Kimisis tis Theotokou** – all built by the venerable Christodoulos.
The Church of **Ag. Ioannis tou Theologou** nestles among the rocks in **Lagoudi** and on May 8th the festival of the patron saint is celebrated, while a large festival with traditional mezedes (hors d'oeuvres) is held on October 26th at the Chapel of Ag. Georgios situated in the forest at **Mavrokambion**.
As time passes, the thought of a swim in the cool waters of the Aegean becomes more and more appealing. The beach at **Tingaki** extends 2 km and is fully organised for all tastes and choices in water sports. Fine white sand inside and outside the water, a sea that deepens gradually and Pserimos lying directly opposite

in an area that obstructs the strong northern winds – all blend together to form a scene from the most popular beach on Kos.

On the same side and just a few kilometres to the south lies another large beach **Marmari** which spreads out its silvery sand before the feet of the visitors. This beach - together with Mastichari which we will meet in the next route- attracts wind-surfers, offering an impressive scene to sun-bathers when the northern winds blow.

You will be able to choose from a variety of accommodations if you decide to remain either in Tingaki or in Marmari, as well as an active nightlife.

Water sports in the cosmopolitan beach at Marmari

76-77. Restful moments in beautiful Tingaki

78-79. Kardamena beach

The scenic beaches of Marmari and Tingaki

JET SKIS

Kos - Pyli - Antimachia Kardamena - Mastichari

3rd Route

Another enjoyable trip into the interior of the island begins by travelling further south. We leave **Pyli** behind us and travel through the centre of the island to Antimachia, one of the less developed tourist villages on Kos.

You can enjoy swimming in the more organised beaches in Kardamena and Mastichari, and with brief stops you can visit the tourist sites in the area.

As in the case of the 2nd Route, we again use the town of Kos as our starting point to head southwest. We pass by Zipari and after a few kilometres we reach the crossroad leading to Pyli. The small artificial lake that is used to irrigate the cultivations

The artificial beach at the crossroad for the village of Pyli

Swimming and water sports in attractive Mastichari

The Iconostasis at the Church Stavros

has been transformed into a small paradise by the ducks and wild canes that grow along its banks.

The first settlement that we come across as we head towards Pyli is **Linopotis**, expropriated land that was ceded to the Italian settlers on Kos. Pyli is one of the oldest areas on the island. According to mythology, Hercules took refuge here as he was being pursued by King Evrypilos of Kos (see Mythology).

We first meet modern Pyli, a charming village with many stone houses and a large square. Just 100 meters from the square is an old spring with six taps from which cool refreshing water gushes out.

An ancient grave lies below the **Church of Stavro**, possibly that of the mythical hero Charmylos. The grave is semi-circular with 12 uniformly sculptured crypts, while the church has built-in pieces of white marble from the Ionian portico that at one time covered the façade of the grave.

Continuing uphill after Pyli, we soon arrive at the foot of Mt. Dikeos and the ruins of the **Byzantine castle** of the old Pyli. The view from the castle is im-pressive as we see the beaches from **Tingaki** all the way to **Mastichari** and from **Pserimo** and

The Grave of Charmylos

Kalymno to the Turkish coastline directly opposite.
The old Church of Ypapantis in Paliopyli has been preserved, its wornout frescos dating back to the 14th C. Other significant findings from this church, which may possibly be parts of the ancient sanctuary of Demeter, are exhibited in the Archaeological Museum in Kos.
Our next stop is **Antimachia**, which is situated almost in the middle of the island near the airport. Antimachia is the transportation and agricultural centre of the region. Its residents are gifted as they have great talent for singing and in dancing, which you can enjoy if you happen to be present at a local festival or celebration.
A visit to the Antimachiotiko Spiti (Home) will give you an idea of how life was living on a farm several decades ago. The well preserved windmill will help you live the atmosphere!
Taking the road to the airport we will come across a signpost that will guide us to the **Venetian Castle**

Old Pyli

The picturesque windmill in Antimachia

in Antimachia via an accessible dirt road. A large section of the walls are in good condition while inside we find two old churches: Ag. Paraskevi - which is open once a year on July 26th- and the ravaged Church of Ag. Nikolaos.

Once we reach Antimachia we are faced with a dilemma: Do we turn northwards to visit Mastichari or southwards towards Kardamena?

Mastichari is a former fishing village that now has a fully developed tourist infrastructure. Its attractive white sand and shallow waters are ideal for children, as there are also many trees towards the back of the beach that offer shade from the hot sun.

Whoever desires the comforts of an organised beach can rent a beach umbrella and lounging chairs on the beach, or else show off your skills in various water sports.

The Castle in Antimachia

The same just about applies for **Kardamena**, with its beautiful sandy beach, and this is basically the reason why this village has transformed into one of the most significant resorts on the island. The village is also renowned for its attractive ceramics and the tasty fruits from its fields – melons and water-melons.

The beach that spreads out on both sides of the village extends for 6 km, so we can therefore chose a site - according to our inclination- that is more secluded or more cosmopolitan. Other than its endless beach, Kardamena also entices the

visitor with its lively nightlife and plethora of restaurants.

Scenic views of the harbour of Kardamena

A castle from the old settlement is situated on a hill to the north of the village, while ruins from the **Temple of Apollo** have also been found here.

This Temple is the oldest on the island and the second in size after the Asklepieion. Other artefacts that were discovered include an ancient Roman theatre and a grave – monuments that link today's

Vibrant nightlife in Kardamena

reality with the ancient Municipality of Alasarniton. A more recent monument is the foundation of the old Christian Basilica Church of Ag. Theotitas.

88-89. Enchanting Kardamena

90-91. Kefalos

POINT ONE
ENTRANCE

Kos - Plaka - South Beaches Ag. Stephanos - Kefalos

4th Route

The 4th and final Route on Kos will lead us to the most virgin land on the island... and possibly the most beautiful. We begin from the town of Kos and reach Antimachia, where at the circular square we turn towards Kefalos, the westernmost settlement on the island.

Just before we leave Antimachia we can make a detour to **Plaka**, where there is a small forest and certain

Spend an afternoon in Ag. Stephanos to sate your senses

The blue-green waters of Kefalos beach

The Basilica of Ag.Stephanos

amenities suitable for a break or a picnic.

Travelling towards **Kefalos** we will pass many crossroads that end up in innumerable beaches in the region. These are small or larger leeward sandy coves that are ideal for swimming and enjoyment of the Greek summer. You will find beach bars or mobile canteens on many of these beaches that offer the swimmers and sunbathers snacks, coffees and... "sfinakia" (chasers).

Paradise is among the most famous and most cosmopolitan beaches, followed by **Ag. Stephanos,** which is the site for **Club Mediterannee.** The ruins of the early Christian Basilica of Ag. Stephanos -with its finely worked ancient mosaics and columns- are situated on a strip of land jutting into the sea.

Cosmopolitan Paradise beach

Close by is the **Church of the Panagia** of Palatiani, built on the site of the ancient acropolis, which offers a scenic view of the **Islet of Kastri** with the white Chapel of Ag. Nikolaos. The ruins of the ancient capital of Astypalea can be found in **Palatia** about 2 km outside Kefalos. Only the foundations of a temple and some sections of the theatre have remained from the ancient city.

Other than the picturesqueness of Kefalos and attractive beaches, western Kos also has many scenic sites to offer its visitors, since this area was the centre

The beaches of Camel and Sunny glitter under the dazzling sun

The Castle in Kefalos

Crystal clear waters in Limniona

of the island during the period of antiquity. Nearby, a cave with prehistoric findings dating back to the Third Millennium B.C. was discovered on the mountain range **of Zini.** This cave was called the Cave of **Aspro Petro** (white rock).

In **Kefalos** it is worth visiting the **Traditional Home** and **"Papa's Mill"** so that you can get an idea of agricultural life several decades ago. Above the village we have the ruins of the **Medieval Castle of the Knights**.

Local belief has it that a dragon lived in this Castle. According to tradition, the goddess Artemis transformed the daughter of Hippocrates into a dragon but gave her one chance to recover her human form; she had to kiss a knight.

Other than the beaches on the western side of Kos, near Kefalos, you may also swim in the secluded beaches of **Ag. Thelogos** in the area of Limniona. On the road to the beach we come across a crossroad leading to the **scenic Monastery of Ag. Ioannis**, where the venerable saint is celebrated in the traditional manner.

A traditional house in the village of Kefalos

98-99. The coastal settlement of Kefalos, with the Castle in the background

Excursions to the nearby islands

Every day small boats sail from the harbour on Kos to the nearby islands of **Kalymnos**, **Pserimos** and **Nisyros**, as well as to the town of **Boundroum** (**Alikarnassos**) that lies opposite on the Turkish coast. But you can also sail from Mastichari to Kalymnos and from Kardamena to Nisyros.

These excursions usually include a light snack and a meal. During your trip to **Kalymnos** you will have the opportunity to visit a traditional sponge factory, while on Nisyros you can see the **volcano** that covers the major part of the island. The excursion to Kalymnos may also include a stopover at Pserimos or the **islet of Plati** for a swim.

Other than these types of excursions, skin-divers may also enjoy their hobby by joining one of the daily outings recommended by the travel agencies and go "fishing" for sponges in the waters of the Dodecanese, always of course accompanied by experienced divers.

Kalymnos, the sponge island

Even though it is still active, the volcano on Nisyros is the chief tourist attraction

Finally, there are also excursions to Rhodes and Patmos -usually once a week- that are organised by some travel agencies. However, since the distances to these islands are quite far, you should therefore visit one of the travel agencies situated along the coastal road (Kountouriotis St.) and see the programs that they offer.
Let us however take a brief look at these three islands that are popular with those visiting Kos.

KALYMNOS

On Kalymnos the sponge-divers still continue to dive into the deep waters of the Aegean to bring to the surface in their own traditional manner the "fruits" of the sea. Traditions are still very strong on this beautiful Dodecanesean island, bringing to mind the moments when the sponge-boats depart and when they joyously return with a full "crop".
But now tourism has become another source of income

A traditional diving outfit used by sponge-divers

for the inhabitants, who see their island filling every year with more and more foreigners who appreciate serenity and beautiful seas. More visitors pour in everyday via the daily organised excursions from nearby islands.

The small boats take about 2 hours to sail from Kos to Kalymnos. Arriving in the scenic capital of Kalymnos or **Pothia**, we are greeted by the **statue of a mermaid** sitting on the rocks and by the charming houses with their multi-coloured windows, thus giving a very pleasant first impression to the visitor.

It is certain that you will find some time to wander around this hospitable town and visit the **Church of Christ or Sotira** that is situated on the coastal road. The church's iconostasis is a work of art by the renowned Tynian sculpture **Giannouli Chalepa,** with icons and frescoes made by local artists.

Attractive buildings and rich vegetation compose the picture of the harbour. Along the waterfront and the tourist shops the sponges personify Kalymnos, so don't forget to visit the sponge processing factories. If you still have some spare time, go and visit the interesting exhibits at the Archaeological – Folkloric Museum. We'll come across the **Castle of Chrisocheria** just outside the town, built by the Knights of Rhodes upon ancient and Byzantium ruins, with the Chapel of Chrisochera inside it. Chorio is the old capital of the island, and here the Knights also left their mark by reinforcing the Byzantine Pera Castle.

PSERIMOS

The majority of the organised excursions combine a visit to Kalymnos with a stopover for a swim in the translucent waters of **Pserimos**. Its chief attraction is the attractive beaches that can be found

The statue of the mermaid in the harbour.

Swimming in the blue waters of Massouri

The village of Pali in Nisyros

throughout the island. All those who truly desire a quiet holiday can stay in one of the few rooms that are available on the island.

NISYROS

Formed from volcano eruptions, Nisyros is a place of wild beauty. This is the scientific version because mythology refers to its own version. Thus according to mythology, during the period of the Gigantomachy (war of the Giants) Poseidon (the god of the sea) plucked a rock from Kos and in anger threw it at the giant Polyvotis with the intention of killing him. This rock, which crushed the giant, became Nisyros, and the half-dead giant shakes the earth every now and then with his groans, thus awakening the volcano.
The capital and harbour of the island **is Mandraki**, with its white houses spread out below the imposing rock containing the Monastery of the **Panagia Spiliani**, while dominating the harbour from a height of 150 m is

the Castle of Spiliani, a memento from the passing of the Knights. The view from here is unique as it hugs the harbour, adjacent shores with their black volcanic rocks and the islets of **Gyali**, **Pergousa**, **Strongyli** and **Pachia** in the background.

In the courtyard of the Castle we have the **Monastery of the Panagia** (Virgin Mary), the patron saint of the island, in the same site where around the 4th Century B.C. there were the walls of the old city and the remains of temples and ancient cemetaries.

The buses that travel to the volcano start off from the waterfront. While travelling to mountainous picturesque village of **Nikia**, we meet the impressive **volcano crater** in the area of **Lakki**. The vegetation becomes less and less and the scenery more dry and wild as we approach the crater.

The centre of the island is the semi-active main crater that was formed by the volcano erupting 24,000 years ago, covering the sides of the island with a layer of pumice-stones 100 meters thick.

One of the three craters of the volcano –with a diameter of 260 m and a depth of 30 m- opens before our feet,

Beautiful Mandraki

causing a feeling a awe to all those present. The path trails down to the craterbed where sulphur steams out of little holes in the earth (which the locals call "xefisistres" or safety valve), thus scattering its pungent smell into the atmosphere.
You were probably warned by the travel agency that it would be preferable if you wore mountain boots or shoes with thick soles because the high temperatures

A picturesque house in Nisyros

that developed at the bottom of the crater were capable of melting rubber soles.
Without fail, your visit to Nisyros will remain an unforgettable experience.

The residents of Kalymnos have been diving for sponges since the days of Antiquity

EXCURSION TO TURKEY

About once a week excursion boats sail from Kos to the Turkish coast that lies opposite. The nearest town is **Boundroum** (or Alikarnassos in ancient times). Excursions from Turkey arrive at Kos with the same frequency in order to see the beautiful island of Hippocrates.

Alikarnassos is situated on the Asia Minor coast opposite Kalymnos. In Antiquity Alikarnassos was known as the birthplace of Herodotus and as the site of the "Mausoleum", one of the seven wonders of the world. Fragments from this grand tomb, which had been built for King Mausolos, came to light in the 1850's. Unfortunately, only a few traces of the monuments of Antiquity have been found in Boundroum.

In contrast, the Castle built by the Knights of St. John in the 15th C. is well-preserved. The Castle was dedicated to St. Peter and is known as Petronion. With the passing of time the Turkish residents renamed it Boundroum in a corruption of its initial name.

The Castle is built on a rock that juts into the water, with strong walls and a triple moat. On the walls we can see the coat of arms and the escutcheon of the families of the Knights.

Moments from the daily life of a fisherman

KEY - ΥΠΟΜΝΗΜΑ
Main Asphalt Road
Κεντρικός Άσφαλτος
Asphalt Road
Άσφαλτος
Earth Road
Χωματόδρομος
Rough Earth Road
Δύσβατος Χωματόδρομος
Inhabited Area
Κατοικημένη Περιοχή
Monastery
Μοναστήρι
Archeological Site
Αρχαιολογικός Χώρος
Cave
Σπήλαιο
Castle
Κάστρο
Airport
Αεροδρόμιο
Beach
Παραλία
Port
Λιμάνι
N. K
KOS
ΙΚΑΡΙΟ ΠΕΛΑΓΟΣ
IKARIO SEA
ΜΑΣΤΙΧΑΡΙ
MASTICHARI
Αντιμάχεια
Andimahia
ΟΡΜΟΣ ΧΟΧΥΛΑΡΙΟΥ
HOHILARI BAY
ΟΡΜΟΣ ΔΑΦΝΗΣ
DAFNI BAY
ΟΡΜΟΣ ΜΗΛΙΟΥ
MILIOS BAY
Ακ. Χιώνες
C. Chones
ΑΓ.ΣΤΕΦΑΝΟΣ
AG.STEFANOS
Μηλιές
Milies
Κροτήρι
Krotiri
ΚΕΦΑΛΟΣ
KEFALOS
Ακ. Συκοφιά
C. Sikoia
ΚΑΜΑΡΙ
KAMARI
ΚΟΛΠΟΣ ΚΕΦΑΛΟΥ
GULF OF KEFALOS
Ζηνί
Zini
Ακ. Κατά
C. Kata
Ακ. Ρούθιανο
C. Routhiano
ΝΙΣΥΡΟΣ
NISSIROS
Μ.Αγ.Ιωάννη
M.Ag.Ioani
Λάθρα
Lathra
ΟΡΜΟΣ ΣΚΙΝΟΥ
SKINOS BAY
ΚΑΡΠΑΘΙΟ Π
KARPATHIC
ΟΡΜΟΣ ΧΙΛΑΝΔΡΙΟΥ
HILANDRI BAY
Ακ. Κρίκελλο
C. Krikelo
ΟΡΜΟΣ ΜΟΣΧΑΛΙΟΥ
MOSHALI BAY

Ακ. Αμμουδιά
C. Amoudia
ΠΕΙΡΑΙΑΣ
PIRAEUS
ΛΑΜΠΗ
LAMPI
ΚΩΣ
KOS
ΟΡΜΟΣ ΚΩ
KOS BAY
ΡΟΔΟΣ
RHODES
ΨΑΛΙΔΙ
PSALIDI
Ακ. Λούρος
C. Louros
ΤΙΓΚΑΚΙ
TIGAKI
ΑΡΙ
ARI
Πλατάνι
Platani
Παραδείσι
Paradisi
Ζηπάρι
Zipari
ΑΣΚΛΗΠΙΕΙΟ
ASKLEPIEION
Άγ.Φωκάς
Ag.Fokas
Ακ. Άγ.Φωκάς
C. Ag.Fokas
Τροτσούλι
Trotsouli
ΕΜΠΡΟΣ ΘΕΡΜΗ
EBROS THERMI
Λαγούδι
Lagoudi
Ασφενδιού
Asfendiou
Αμανιού
Amaniou
Πυλί
Pili
Άγ.Δημήτριος
Ag.Dimitrios
Σελλάδι
Seladi
Ζιά
Zia
Όρος Δίκαιος
Dikeos Mt.
Παλαιό Πυλί
Old Pili
ΠΙΣΩ ΘΕΡΜΗ
PISO THERMI
Κουβάς
Kouvas
Ακάκι
Akaki
N
W
E
S
ΚΑΡΔΑΜΑΙΝΑ
KARDAMENA
ΤΟΣ
Α
Ν. ΣΤΡΟΓΓΥΛΗ
SROGILI IS.
Ν. ΠΑΧΕΙΑ
PAHIA IS.
Ν. ΝΙΣΥΡΟΣ
NISSIROS IS.
ΚΑΡΠΑΘΙΟ ΠΕΛΑΓΟΣ
KARPATHIO SEA
Πάλοι
Pali
ΜΑΝΔΡΑΚΙ
MANDRAKI
Λουτρά
Loutra
Εμπορειός
Emporios
Προφ. Ηλίας
Prof.Ilias
ΗΦΑΙΣΤΕΙΟ
VOLCANO
Νικιά
Nikia
M.Panagias Kiras
M.Ag.Ioanou
Ακ. Κατέρο
C. Katero
ΟΡΜΟΣ ΚΟΡΦΟΣ
KORFOS BAY
Ακ. Λευκός
C. Lefkos
ΟΡΜΟΣ ΛΕΥΚΟΣ
LEFKOS BAY
Αυλάκι
Avlaki
ΟΡΜΟΣ ΓΡΑΝΑ
GRANA BAY
Ακ. Αυλάκι
C. Avlaki

HOTELS

ΚΩΣ - KOS

ΑΓ.ΦΩΚΑΣ -AG.FOKAS

DIMITRA BEACH	22420.28581

ΗΡΑΚΛΗΣ - IRAKLIS

KONI- DORIS	22420.26518

ΚΑΡΔΑΜΑΙΝΑ - KARDAMENA

AKTI	22420.92777
DAEDALOS	22420.58500
LAKITIRA	22420.91537
LANGAS AEGEAN VILLAGE	22420.91401
LOUIS HELIOS BEACH	22420.91602
NORIDA BEACH	22420.91230
PORTO BELLO BEACH	22420.91193
KARDA BEACH	22420.91221
KALIMERA KOS	22420.91591
KARMELINA	-
KRISMARI	22420.91642
RIO	22420.91627
SILVER BEACH	22420.91415
SUNNY VIEW	22420.91028
AGRELIS	22420.91126
ALMA	22420.91365
ANDAVIS	22420.91461
ANGELIKI	22420.91358
CHRISTINA BEACH	22420.91326
KLEOPATRA	22420.91181
DIMIMAR	-
ELGA	-
HARIKLIA	-
INO	-
KALIA APARTMENTS	-
KALOXENIA	22420.91112
KAMARES	22420.91091
KARDAMENA	22420.91252
KARDAMOS	22420.91323
LYDIA	-
MAMOUZELOS	22420.91467
MARIGO	22420.22544
MIKARGY	22420.91492
NIKOLAOU	-
NIKOLIOS	-
NISSIA	22420.91091
PERIVOLI	22420.91105
SEVA	-
SILVER BEACH 2	22420.91415
SUNBEAM	22420.91522
VALINAKIS BEACH	22420.91354
VARKAS	22420.91517
VERGINA	22420.28132
VILLA PADAROTA	22420.91134
ARGYRI	22420.91292

ΚΕΦΑΛΟΣ - KEFALOS

KARLOS VILLAGE	22420.71213
ANTHOULA	22420.71339
ATHINOULA	22420.72184
ELENI	-
ΙΟΝΙΚΟΣ	22420.71166
KAMARI BAY	22420.71556
KOKALAKIS BEACH	22420.71466
KORDISTOS	22420.71251
ZEUS	22420.71590
SIDNEY	-
MARIA	22420.71308

ΚΩΣ - KOS

AEGEON	22420.24701
CONTINENTAL PALACE	22420.22737
AGHIOS CONSTANTINOS	22420.23301
ALEXANDRA	22420.28301
ANGELA	22420.21246
ARTEMIS	22420.23313
ASTRON	22420.23703
CHEVALIERS	22420.23503
GALLIA	22420.23230
GIASSEMI	-
IRIS	22420.24454
KOS	22420.22480
MARINA	22420.25111
POLINA	22420.25969
THEOXENIA	22420.22310
ADONIS	-
AFENTOULIS	22420.25321
AFRODITI	-
AKTAEON APARTMENTS	22420.24977
ALCYON	22420.23739
ALEXANDRA 2	22420.25202
ALIKI	22420.24198
AMERIKANA	22420.22947
ANASTASIA	22420.28598
ANNE	22420.23030
ANNETA	22420.24031
APOLLONIA	22420.25653
ASPA HOLIDAYS	22420.28394
ASTERIAS	22420.23665
BAHAMES	22420.24374
BRISTOL	22420.22865
CAPTAINS	22420.22961
CARAVEL	-
CONSTANTIA	22420.28244
COS SUNSMILE	22420.25607
COSTEL	22420.22969
DELFINI	22420.28802
DIMITRIS PARITSA	22420.24673
EFTIXIA	22420.26051
EKATERINI	22420.28285
ELLI	22420.28401
ELMA	22420.22920
ESPERIDES	-
FALIRON	-
FANTASSIA	22420.23922
FILOXENIA	22420.22144
GALAXIAS	22420.23361
GALAZIOS OURANOS	22420.22090
GALINI	22420.23368
GEORGE	22420.23297
GOLDEN CITY	22420.23057
HELLAS	22420.23017
IBISCUS	22420.22214
IMPERIAL	22420.23800
INTERNATIONAL	22420.23751
IPOKRATIS	22420.23221
KAMELIA	22420.28983
KARIS	22420.22990
KENTRO AG. MARINA	22420.25429
KOALA	22420.22897
KONDIA BEACH	22420.22663
KONI	22420.23913
KOS BAY	22420.26126
MANOS	22420.28931
MARIE	22420.22291
MARITINA	22420.23241
MARITON APARTMENTS	22420.25875
MERSINI	22420.22602
MESSOGHIOS	22420.23161
MOUZAKIS A	22420.25891
NIRIIDES BEACH	22420.23380
OLGA	22420.22694
OLIMPIA	22420.22812
OSCAR	22420.28090
PARADISSOS	22420.22988
PARITSA	22420.28971
PAVLOS	22420.23151
PHAETHON	22420.28901
PHANTASIA	22420.23922
POSSIDON	22420.23365

HOTELS

ΚΩΣ - KOS

SEMIRAMIS	22420.26655
SOLEIL APARTMENTS	22420.28290
THEONIA	22420.23303
THOMAS	22420.24646
VERONIKI	22420.28122
VIRGINIA	22420.23749
ZEPHYROS	22420.22245
ZIKAS	22420.23827
AFROS	22420.25333
DODECANESSUS	22420.28460
HELENA	22420.22740
ALEXIS	22420.28798
CHRISTINA	22420.22466
ORION	22420.28482

ΜΑΣΤΙΧΑΡΙ - MASTIHARI

ACHILEFS BEACH	22420.59160
KANARI BEACH	22420.59132
MASTIHARI BAY	22420.59300
NEPTUNE BEACH	22420.41480
NEPTUNE VILLAGE RESIDENCE	22420.41785
PRINCESS OF KOS	22420.41524
COUROS CLUB	22420.59214
KARANTONIS	22420.59076
ARANT	22420.51167
LOUIS	22420.59094
MASTIHARI BEACH	22420.59252
THALASSIA AVRA	22420.59171
WAVE (Kyma)	22420.51545
FAENARETI	22420.51395
ZEVGAS	22420.23012
SEAGULL'S BAY	22420.59294
ILIOLOUSTES MERES	22420.69091
IPANEMA	22420.69194
KALOUDIS	22420.69757
MARIANA	22420.69090
MENI BEACH	22420.69217
MYROS	22420.29768
ODESSA	-
PAXINOS	22420.69306
STARLY BLUE SKY	22420.69586
SUNSET	22420.69428
TROPICAL SOL	22420.69341

ΨΑΛΙΔΙ - PSALIDI

ALBATROS BEACH	22420.23381
KYPRIOTIS - PANORAMA	22420.57000
ARCHIPELAGOS	22420.23408
ARISTO	22420.21306
HIPOKRATES PALACE	22420.24401
KYPRIOTIS VILLAGE	22420.27640
OCEANIS	22420.24641
PLATANISTA	22420.27551
RAMIRA BEACH	22420.22891
SUN PALACE	22420.24530
ALEXANDRA BEACH	22420.27791
ANDROMEDA	22420.29886
THEODOROU BEACH	22420.22280
ENTMARK	22420.25952
MARITINA MARE	22420.24801
PALM BEACH	22420.21771

ΜΑΡΜΑΡΙ - MARMARI

ANGELA MARE	22420.41622
KARAVIA BEACH	22420.41291
PARADISE PHAETHON BEACH	22420.41488
BOURADANIS VILLAGE	22420.68190
ESPERIA	22420.42010
GIAKALIS	22420.41586
MARILIZA	22420.41433
MARMARI BEACH	22420.4100
NINA	22420.41590
PALADION BUNGALOWS	22420.41407
PILI BAY	22420.41211
ROSELAND	22420.41650
SANDI BEACH	22420.414262

ΜΑΡΜΑΡΙ - MARMARI

STELLA MARIS	22420.41003
TONIS	22420.41457
ANTHIA	22420.23393
ASLANIS VILLAGE	22420.41796
BLUE JAY	22420.41533
GIANNIS	22420.68187
ERMIS	-
NOBEL	22420.41003

ΛΑΜΠΗ - LAMPI

AEOLOS BEACH	22420.26781
ATLANTIS	22420.28731
PELAGOS	22420.30011
APELLIS	22420.24629
APOLLON	22420.27331
KALYPSO	22420.23552
COSMOPOLITAN	22420.23411
COSTA-ANTZELA	22420.25800
DIMITRIOS	22420.27680
THALASSA	22420.29614
ALICE SPRINGS	22420.23473
ARGO	22420.24375
ATHINA	22420.25044
ATLANTIS 2	22420.23755
BOEME	22420.26381
COLUMBIA BEACH	22420.28440
FROSSINI	22420.25231
GAYA	22420.25804
HOTEL BEACH BLUE SEA	22420.26280
IRENE	22420.28186
LAURA	22420.28981
PANTELIS	22420.25456
SMARAGDI	22420.23380

ΤΙΓΚΑΚΙ - TINGAKI

KOS PALACE	22420.69890
TINGAKI BEACH	22420.69446
KONSTANTINOS ILIOS 2	22420.69411
CORALI	22420.68212
GAYA VILLAGE 1	-
GAYA VILLAGE 2	22420.68332
GOLDEN STAR	22420.69291
IRINA BEACH	22420.69850
OASIS	22420.69068
PARK LANE	22420.29170
TINGAKIS STAR	22420.69541
ANGELA	22420.68357
ARAMNI	22420.69964
ARIADNI	22420.69003
ASPRO SPITI	22420.69296
CONSTANTINOS ILIOS	22420.69411
DIMIS BEACH	22420.68172
FILIO	22420.69133
GOLDEN SUN	22420.69172
HOLYWOOD	22420.69206

ΝΙΣΥΡΟΣ NISSIROS

ΜΑΝΔΡΑΚΙ - MANDRAKI

POLYVOTIS	22420.31011
HARITOS	22420.31322
PORFYRIS	22420.31376
TA LOTRIDIA	22420.31237
WHITE BEACH	22420.31497

USEFUL INFORMATION

ΑΣΤΥΝΟΜΙΑ		**POLICE**
Κως	22420.22100	Kos
Νίσυρος	22420.31201	Nissiros
Κέφαλος	22420.71222	Kefalos
Πυλί	22420.41222	Pyli
Αντιμάχεια	22420.51222	Andimahia
ΤΟΥΡΙΣΤΙΚΗ ΑΣΤΥΝΟΜΙΑ		**TOURIST POLICE**
Κως	22420.26666	Kos
ΛΙΜΕΝΑΡΧΕΙΟ		**PORT AUTHORITY**
Κως	22420.26594	Kos
Νίσυρος	22420.31222	Nissiros
Πειραιάς	210.4226000	Piraeus
ΝΟΣΟΚΟΜΕΙΟ		**HOSPITAL**
Κως	22420.22300	Kos
	22420.28050	
ΙΑΤΡΕΙΑ		**FIRST AID STATION**
Ζηπάρι	22420.69202	Zipari
Καρδάμαινα	22420.91202	Kardamena
Αντιμάχεια	22420.51230	Antimahia
Κέφαλος	22420.71230	Kefalos
Πυλί	22420.41230	Pili
Νίσυρος	22420.31217	Nissiros
ΜΟΥΣΕΙΑ		**MUSEUMS**
Αρχαιολογικό Κως	22420.28326	Archeological Kos
Ασκληπιείο	22420.28763	Asklipiio
Ρωμαϊκή Οικία	22420.23234	Casa Romana
ΝΟΜΑΡΧΕΙΑ		**PREFECTURE**
Δωδεκαννήσου (Ρόδος)	22410.46500	Dodekanissa (Rhodes)
Επαρχείο Κως	22420.27477	Kos
ΠΥΡΟΣΒΕΣΤΙΚΗ		**FIRE DEPARTMENT**
Κως	22420.22199	Kos
ΥΠΕΡΑΣΤΙΚΑ ΛΕΩΦ. (ΚΤΕΛ)	**22420.22292**	**INTERCITY BUS STATION**
ΑΣΤΙΚΑ ΛΕΩΦ. (ΔΕΑΣ)	**22420.26276**	**CITY BUS**
ΤΡΑΙΝΑΚΙΑ	**22420.26276**	**MINI TRAINS**
ΤΑΞΙ		**TAXI**
Κως (πόλη)	22420.22777	Kos (city)
	22420.23333	
Νίσυρος	22420.31460	Nissiros
ΑΕΡΟΔΡΟΜΙΟ	**22420.51229**	**AIRPORT**
ΟΛΥΜΠΙΑΚΗ	22420.28331	OLYMPIC AIRWAYS
ΠΡΟΞΕΝΕΙΑ		**CONSULATES**
Μ. Βρετανίας	22420.21549	G. Britain
Δανίας	22420.23301	Denmark
Φιλανδίας	22420.22340	Finland
Ιταλίας	22420.21991	Italy
Σουηδίας	22420.26278	Sweden